The Art Of Becoming Ushers & Greeters Of Excellence: A Training Manual For Ministry Today

Dedications

To My Wife Toby Lynne Gillespie-Mobley Who

Encouraged Me Begin To Write And Continues To

Pray For Me. She Is My Best Friend

To The Ushers and Greeter Of Roxbury

Presbyterian Church, Glenville New Life

Community Church, New Life Fellowship,

Calvary Presbyterian Church & New Life At

Calvary Whom I Have Had The Privilege Of

Training Over Three Decades Of Ministry

To God For The Gifts He Gives To Me To Pass To

Others

Table Of Contents

Meet The Author

Rick Gillespie-Mobley has been a committed evangelical pastor since 1983. He currently is a part of A Covenant Order Of Evangelical Presbyterians (ECO). He is a gifted communicator and uses stories and humor in his messages in a way that engages his audiences. He has an extensive Christian background in several Christian denominations that include charismatics, Methodists, Church of God In Christ, Full Gospel, United Church of Christ, Assemblies of God and Presbyterians.

Rick has a true love for the church of Jesus Christ and wants to help each church become all that it can be. He has trained ushers and greeters for over three decades of ministry. He loves helping people to discover their gifts and to put them into practice in the body of Christ.

Rick was married on August 30, 1980 to his bride Toby. They have served together as co-pastors for nearly 30 years. In addition to their adult children Samantha, Anita, Keon, and Sharon, they have served as foster parents for 20 years. Rick is a graduate of Hornell Senior High School in Hornell, NY, Hamilton College B.A. in Clinton, NY, Gordon Conwel Theological Seminary M. Div. in S. Hamilton, MA, Trinity Bible College & Seminary D. Min in Newburgh , IN and Boston University School of Law J.D in Boston, MA.

Rick has served with his wife Toby as co-pastors of Roxbury Presbyterian Church (6 years) in Boston, Ma, Glenville New Life Community Church (24 years) in Cleveland, Oh, New Life Fellowship (4 Years) in Cleveland, OH, Calvary Presbyterian Church (2 years) in Cleveland, OH. Since September 2013 they have been serving together on a pastoral team with Kellie Sullivan and Willie Nieves at New Life At Calvary in

Cleveland, OH. New Life Calvary is a merger of Glenville New Life Community Church and Calvary Presbyterian Church. Rick and Toby were both ordained in the Presbyterian Church of the United States of America, but have since transferred their membership to A Covenant Order of Evangelical Presbyterian (ECO). Rick was admitted to practice law in both Massachusetts and Ohio.

Rick has written several e-books including "The Art Of Writing A Eulogy", "Easter Comes Alive: Six Sermons For Holy Week, and "Rich Black History Sermons: Africans In The Bible." Rick dibbles and dabbles with photography and enjoys working with computers. He can be found on the shores of Lake Erie where he goes to meet with his God. He enjoys quiet evenings at home with his wife watching sci-fi and police drama TV programs.

What's Your Heart's Motivation

Psalm 84:10 (KJV) [10] *For a day in thy courts is better than a thousand. I had rather be a doorkeeper in the house of my God, than to dwell in the tents of wickedness.*

You are most likely reading this book because you want to excel at the ministry of hospitality by serving well as an usher or greeter in your church. You have chosen a very high calling for ministry. Roman 12:8 encourages us to practice hospitality. As an usher or a greeter, you are given the privilege of offering hospitality to others. Keep in mind that Jesus told us, that whatever we do for the least of his brothers and his sisters, we do for Him.

David reveals in Psalm 84:10 that one of the most important places one could serve is in the doorway of the house of the Lord. He would rather serve in God's house more than in any place that those outside of God had to offer to him. He even considers it a privilege just to be in the house of the Lord by stating that just one day in the house of the Lord is better than a thousand days elsewhere.

Excellent ushers and greeters are two of the pillars of every great church. One of the things that made Jesus so unique was his ability to make everyone feel welcomed in his presence. From the leper who returned to say thank you, to the rich and powerful Zacchaeus who came down from the tree, from the Samaritan woman who had her prejudices, to the sinful woman who anointed Jesus feet with perfume and wiped them with her hair, and from the uneducated fisherman Peter who left all to follow him, to the highly educated pharisee, Joseph of Arimathea who buried him, Jesus made them all feel welcomed. Jesus loved people.

One of the things those desiring to be ushers and greeters must ask themselves is, "Do I really love people?" An usher and greeter are called to show love and respect in a slightly higher way than those just sitting in the pews. Ushers and greeters remember at all times Jesus' call to love thy neighbor as thyself. Are you willing to love those of all ages who enter the house of the Lord? Are you prejudiced in any way toward or against the poor or the rich?

Can you accept the person with spiked purple hair with 10 pairs of earrings on her face just as easily as you can the 65 year old man in his nice blue suit? Can you love the person who does not smell too nice? Can you avoid letting a person's ethnic background keep you from treating that person a certain way? Excellent ushers and greeters are no respecter of persons in the love they demonstrate toward people of different backgrounds.   They take their post with the knowledge of Galatians 3:28 which let us know that in Christ, there is neither Jew nor Greek, male nor female, slave nor free, but that we are all one.

Jesus told potential disciples that if they would come and follow Him, he would make them fishers of people.   Excellent ushers and greeters understand that they are to be fishers of men and women as they carry out their duties. You never know who God is going to send into the church or where a person is on the continuum of coming to know God. Ushers and greeters play a crucial part in helping a person get closer to God.

The love of Christ which radiates from ushers and greeters may be part of the bait that God is using to catch fish which are passing through the church. Keep in mind that there are plenty of fish that enter the church that still need to be caught. Usher and greeters should pray before taking their posts, "Lord, use me to help catch fish today."

There have been many Sundays in which I have asked guests, "who invited you to church today?", and the response has been "no one, I was just passing by and felt I should go in." God sends fish into the church, and the first person God usually sends them to is an usher or greeter. Excellent ushers and greeters are helping to determine people's eternal destiny Sunday after Sunday. That is why being an usher or greeter is so very important. Each time you do your job well, you help to advance the kingdom of God. Your ministry has eternal dividends attached to it.

The Invitation

Proverbs 18:24 (KJV)[24] A man that hath friends must shew himself friendly: and there is a friend that sticketh closer than a brother.

In chapter 22 of Matthew's gospel, Jesus told the story of a king who issued an invitation to guests to come and attend a banquet that he was preparing for his son. Many of those invited did not want to attend, so the king sent his servants into streets and country lanes to find anyone they could to invite them to the banquet. Each time believers gather for a worship service, an invitation has been extended to people to come and celebrate by worshipping the King of Kings and the Lord of Lords. That invitation is extended to those who are in the streets and in the country lanes who may not at all be familiar with the King or know the proper etiquette for being in the King's presence. They may even unsure of exactly what the palace of the King is going to look like.

Excellent ushers and greeters prepare people to feel welcome after they have accepted the invitation to come. As people arrive at a church for the first time, they really do not know what is on the other side of the door leading into the church. They are not sure, what the people will be like, where to go, or what exactly to expect. It is often said, "You only get one chance to make a good first impression." Chances are, the first impression a guests gets from the church is usually going to come from an encounter with an usher or greeter.

Once again this is why excellent ushers and greeters are two of the pillars of a successful and healthy church. They help influence and determine what people think about the rest of the people in the church. A kind and warm reception by an usher or greeter puts the guest in the mindset of expecting others in the church to also be warm and kind. Unfortunately a cold and rude reception at the hands of an usher or greeter may cause the person to feel that others in the church will offer similar treatment. The person may be thinking, "What on earth have I gotten myself into this time."

Therefore ushers and greeters must accept the responsibility that goes along with being them being the people who have the privilege of making a positive first impression. The reception the guest receives is going to help shape the person's attitude toward the rest of the people in the church. More importantly that initial reaction may partially determine the person's attitude in being able to engage in worship. Many churches may have a meet and greet time in the service in which members are encouraged to turn and greet one another. This part of the service will seem very natural if the person has had a positive experience with an usher or greeter. But if the experience with an usher or greeter has been a negative one, this part of the service may seem somewhat phony to the guest.

Excellent ushers and greeters have the ability to make people feel welcome the moment they enter the church. A simple smile and a joyful greeting can go a long way. It is not just the guest, who comes to your church that needs a warm welcome. The members who come week after week can also have their spirits lifted by the warmth and kindness of an usher or greeter.

It has been said, that if you really want to have a lot of people at your funeral, be one of the most welcoming ushers or greeters in your church. Everyone will know who you are by name. You will be talked about in a positive way at more family Sunday dinners than you can imagine. People love people who take the time to give them that little extra pick up in their spirits. You have been empowered by God to help make people feel welcomed.

Entering The Unknown

Genesis 28:16 (KJV) [16] *And Jacob awaked out of his sleep, and he said, Surely the LORD is in this place; and I knew it not.*

We live in a time in which there are more and more people who have grown up without ever going inside of a church. I can recall at one Vacation Bible School event a little boy asked me, "Are you the president of this place?" He had no concept of what a pastor was. Those who are in the church for a while, begin to think that everyone knows what takes place in church and what is going to happen during the service. The reality may be just the opposite. The person may be entering completely unknown territory.

Just think what it would be like for you if you went into a Buddhist Temple or Muslim Mosque for the first time. What feelings do you think would be going through your mind? Would you be thinking about not sticking out like a sore thumb? Would you be hoping not to do anything that might offend someone? Would you know where to sit or not to sit?

What would make you feel more secure having entered the doors? What if you had entered by yourself, and there was no one to give you any directions? What if you really had to go to the bathroom before you went into the service, would you even know where to begin to look? Would you feel okay just wandering through the building on your own? What would you need to feel more comfortable?

If you answered some of the questions that have just been listed in the paragraph above, you will have gone through the experience of many visitors that may enter your church. I like to think of it as having experienced "Visitor Shock." When guests arrive for the first time, many of them do not know all the unwritten rules and directions that are a part of your church. Every church has them whether they are aware of them are not.

In some churches, the direction to the sanctuary is immediately visible, but in other churches like the one I serve it is not. To get into our sanctuary after coming through the entrance door from the parking lot, the sanctuary is straight ahead through two French doors, then a right across a large fellowship hall, then a left through two double doors, down the ramp past the chapel, then take a slight right through two different doors with a small lobby in between the doors, and then you enter the sanctuary. To make matters worse, you enter the sanctuary from the front with everyone looking at you as you enter. Our church would be virtually impossible for a first time guests to navigate on their own without a few mistakes just trying to find the sanctuary. Getting to the nursery and youth church is another battle in itself. What are the unwritten directions in your church to get to the sanctuary or the bathrooms?

Having ushers and greeters located at each one of those turns and twists to get to the sanctuary is very important in making the guests feel welcomed and expected. It is very important having an usher or greeter to walk with the guests into the sanctuary, since the eyes of the congregation are upon them as they enter. This is a lot more intimidating than being able to enter the sanctuary from the rear of the sanctuary.

Excellent ushers and greeters attempt to discover the unwritten rules and directions that exist in their church so that they can put themselves in the place of their guest. The guest is thinking, "I do not know where to go. I do not want to look out of place. I do not want to be embarrassed. I do not know what to expect in this service." If the guests have been to other churches, they may also be thinking, "I hope someone tells me about the Nursery if there is one", or "where I should take my children."

Ushers and greeters are there to help guests navigate through the unknown rules and directions of the church. Your presence is usually more valuable than you think it is. You have the honor of being the eyes and helping hands of our local church.

The Servant's Heart

John 13:14-15 (KJV) [14] *If I then, your Lord and Master, have washed your feet; ye also ought to wash one another's feet.* [15] *For I have given you an example, that ye should do as I have done to you.*

Jesus was speaking to his disciples one day about a story in which a master told his servants to get his food ready, and after they had taken care of his needs, they themselves could eat. Jesus then posed the question, "Would you expect the master to then thank the servants for doing what he asked of them?" Given the circumstances and the difference in the relationship between the servants and the master, the answer was an obvious no. Jesus then told the disciples that when they have done what he asked them to do, they should likewise respond by saying, "We really have not done anything that special, we were only doing our duty"

Ushers and greeters are most effective when they recognize they are servants of Jesus Christ, who have been given the opportunity to work on his behalf. His command was to love others by showing them the love of God regardless of their appearance, their background, or their social status. Excellent servants are going to anticipate the needs of those being served. The same is true of excellent ushers and greeters. They have hearts which eagerly anticipate ways in which they can be a blessing to others. This requires ushers and greeters to be attentive to the needs of others.

To meet this requirement, it is very important for ushers and greeters to be at their assigned post. Remember there are several factors that determine how many ushers and greeters you will need. You must consider the number of entrances into the building, the pathway from the entrance to the sanctuary, the number of aisles in your sanctuary, and the number of people attending the service. There should be some way for guests to identify ushers and greeters. It can be something as simple as a badge, a ribbon, or color scheme in dress. It makes it easier for guest to identify you and come to you for assistance or to ask you questions. They expect you will be able to answer their questions or be able to direct them to someone who can.

Ushers and greeters are to be actively involved in looking for the person who may need some assistance. They are looking for the person who enters the building and looks unsure of where to go. They are looking for the people in service who somehow managed to get by without receiving a church bulleting or program and then taking the initiative to get a program or bulletin to them. They are searching for the people, who may need a fan because it is too warm in the building. They are seeking the people who may need a tissue because of tears at a funeral service or because of coughing in the service.

They are looking for people who are unsure of where they should sit in the sanctuary. If the ushers know that a certain section of the church seating is rarely used, they should alert guests who may choose that section to the reality that it might be better for them to sit in a different section with an explanation why. You want to do your part in making sure guests do not experience embarrassment because they did not know some unwritten rule. Ushers and greeters are looking for parents with small kids to let them know of the nursery. If kids go straight to a kids section of the church, excelling ushers and greeters make that known to the person before the person enters the sanctuary.

It is a good idea for ushers and greeters to have cards that explain the nursery or the kid's church program. If your church has a policy for parents with babies, it should be presented to the parents before they enter the sanctuary and let the parents know what options are available to them. Remember, the way you present the information to the parents is going to make all the difference in the way they respond to you. We are called to speak the truth in love. Keep in mind Colossians 3:17, which reminds us that whatever we are doing, regardless of how big or insignificant it may seem, we are to do it to the glory of our Lord Jesus Christ.

The 10 Commandments Of Ushers And Greeters

Deuteronomy 6:17 (KJV) [17] *Ye shall diligently keep the commandments of the LORD your God, and his testimonies, and his statutes, which he hath commanded thee.*

Commandment number one is "You Shall Speak To People." It is amazing how often ushers and greeters overlook this commandment. You should never hand a person a program or a bulletin without speaking to the person with a good morning or good afternoon. Ushers and greeters should speak as pleasantly as possible to both guests and to regular attenders of the church.

Commandment number two is "You Shall Smile At People." The smile is virtually a universal sign of acceptance and welcome. Smiles are absolutely free. Every usher and greeter should be prepared to give away an abundance of smiles each time they serve in their position. People feel more comfortable approaching a person who has a pleasant look on his or her face. Remember, you are radiating the joy of the Lord.

Commandment number three is "You Shall Call People By Their Name Whenever Possible." People enjoy hearing the sound of their name when they arrive at church. It makes them feel loved and accepted. "Good morning, Mrs. Jones" carries a little more weight than simply "good morning." If your church has a church directory, spend some time with the directory and learn the names and faces of as many people as possible. Don't be hesitant to ask people for their names. You can even say, "I may have to ask you your name a few times before I fully remember it, so please bear with me." The people understand you are at least making an attempt to get to know their names. Remember, learning the names of youth is just as important as learning adults. A good usher and greeter does not practice age discrimination.

Commandment number four is "You Shall Be Kind And Helpful." Even when a person is disobeying an unwritten rule, you have got to remember to still be kind and helpful. For instance, many churches have rules as to when a person may enter a service after it has begun. If a person attempts to enter during one of the forbidden moments such as during a prayer or solo, be kind in the way you attempt to prevent the person from entering. Let the person know why you are doing what you are doing and when it is the person may enter.

Commandment number five is "You Shall Have A Genuine Interest In People." As a greeter, do not ask a person, "How Are You Today?" and then move on to the next person before the person has a chance to answer. If you ask the question, be prepared to wait for an answer. If the person indicates he or she is not feeling well, go ahead and offer to pray with them right there on the spot.

It does not have to be a long prayer. Simply asking God to help the person feel better to be able to receive all that God has for them during worship is sufficient. It will also help you to build a better relationship with the person. A huge part of ministry is building relationships. As ushers and greeters, your ministry provides you with a greater opportunity to build relationships with more people, than just about any other ministry. You have the privilege of reaching out to practically everyone in the congregation over a period of time.

Commandment number six is "You Shall Be Generous With Praise." Using phrases such as "It's good to see you", "You're looking great today", and "I'm glad you're a part of our church", can make people look forward to coming to worship. Many people do not receive compliments and affirmations during the week. Ushers and greeters have the privilege of being an affirming person in their lives. You want to remember to keep your compliments appropriate. It is okay to say, "That's a lovely dress" or "that's a nice suit." You should avoid saying things such as, "Wow, you sure look good in that dress" or "you look great in that suit." You do not want to give the impression that you are attempting to flirt with the person.

Commandment number seven is "You Shall Be Alert At All Time." Remember you are seeking ways to be a servant. You are anticipating problems before they happen. You are constantly seeking to enrich someone else's spirit for worship. If you are doing your job in the manner that God intended, you will not be able to get out of the service all that you need. You should consider attending a second service if your church offers one in which you do not serve as an usher or greeter. Or you should watch the service again on DVD or on your church's website if that is an option for you. The price of excelling in your position is you must seek additional opportunities for your own spiritual growth.

Commandment number eight is "You Shall Arrive At Your Post On Time." Your job is one of the most critical ministries in the church. You of all people need to be on time. Many times, guests arrive early at a service and they will need your assistance upon arrival. You cannot provide the assistance if you are not present. Ushers and greeters should be at their post a minimum of fifteen minutes prior to the start of worship.

Commandment number nine is "You Shall Not Hold The Person Present Accountable For People Who Are Missing." It is one thing to ask a woman whose husband is not with her, "How is John today?" It is not appropriate to ask, "Why is John not with you today?" Your job is to affirm the person who is present. Some people will stop attending church if they have to give an account for family members who are no longer attending. It is okay to say something such as, "Please tell John we missed him today." It is not okay to say, "When is John coming back to church?" Ushers and greeters do not want to add guilt to the people they are addressing.

Remember also that when a person returns who has been missing for a while, the correct greeting is "Welcome back home. I'm so glad to see you." The inappropriate greeting is "Where on earth have you been?" Even though your comment may be said in jest, the other person may not take it that way. They may begin to regret coming back because others may respond to them in the same manner. You would be surprised at the number of people who are afraid of rejection if they come to church after having disappeared for weeks or months at a time.

Commandment number ten is "You Shall Not Be Absent From Your Post Without Seeking A Replacement." Church usher and greeter rules will vary on whom to contact when you cannot fulfill your responsibility. Please do not wait until Sunday morning to let the head usher or greeter know you will not be coming in unless it is an emergency. It is often best to try to trade places with another usher or greeter to make sure your post is covered. The ministry that you do is very important in the life of the church. If you can't fulfill your spot on the schedule, let the appropriate person know as soon as possible. The kingdom of God needs faithful and dependable workers.

THE USHERS AND GREETERS 10 COMMANDMENTS

1. You Shall Speak To People.

2. You Shall Smile At People.

3. You Shall Call People By Their Name Whenever Possible.

4. You Shall Be Kind And Helpful.

5. You Shall Have A Genuine Interest In People.

6. You Shall Be Generous With Praise.

7. You Shall Be Alert At All Times.

8. You Shall Arrive At Your Post On Time.

9. You Shall Not Hold The Person Present Accountable For People Who Are Missing.

10. You Shall Not Be Absent From Your Post Without Seeking A Replacement.

10 Fruits That Must Be Eaten

Ephesians 4:30-32 (KJV)[30] And grieve not the holy Spirit of God, whereby ye are sealed unto the day of redemption.[31] Let all bitterness, and wrath, and anger, and clamour, and evil speaking, be put away from you, with all malice: [32] And be ye kind one to another, tenderhearted, forgiving one another, even as God for Christ's sake hath forgiven you.

Not everyone has the right disposition to be a good usher or greeter. In this ministry, personality does indeed matter. But anyone who fully yields themselves to the fruit of the spirit as found in Galatians 5:22-23 can become the kind of servant that God can use in this important ministry. Every usher and greeter should periodically look at themselves in the mirror and measure themselves by the fruits of the spirit.

The first fruit that we find is love. On a scale of 1-10, what do you think is your acceptance rate of others? You should ask a few others what they think your acceptance rate is and compare it to your own number. Sometimes others do not perceive us to be nearly as loving as we think of ourselves as being. The serious look you have on your face, may cause others to believe that you are strict and judgmental, when in fact you may be the very opposite. That is why you want to remember to smile at people.

The second fruit that we find is joy. Do others see you enjoying your role as an usher or greeter? Do you give the appearance that your service is just a job and you wished it was over? Ushers and greeters should have a positive spirit that lifts the hearts of others. David said that he was glad when others invited him to go up to the house of the Lord.

The third fruit we find is peace. As ushers and greeters you are given a certain element of authority within the church. Do you use that authority in such a way to bring peace to situations that could become confrontational? For instance if a group of teenagers are sitting together and talking during the service, do you approach them with a peaceful spirit or an authoritative one? The peace you exemplify will help to bring calmness to a tense situation.

The fourth fruit we find is patience. As ushers and greeters, you must be prepared to encounter some rude and nasty people even within the church. There will be people who are going to defy the authority you have been given. They will insist on entering the service, even when you have told them that now is now the appropriate time. There will even be a few people who have as their aim to irritate you. You must still allow God to work His patience through you so that you do not respond in anger. Remember that you are in the job of dealing with people. People always require patience. Before you give up on someone, please try to remember how often you have asked God to be patient with you.

The fifth fruit we find is kindness. Kindness is more than just being nice. It is being pro-active in doing things for others that need to be done. Reaching down to pick up something someone has dropped is kindness. If you have a bulletin or program that may not be easy to follow, kindness is showing the guest the easiest way to follow the service in the bulletin. Kindness is offering the tissue, offering the fan, or offering the word of prayer. Kindness is taking the person to where the restroom or sanctuary is rather than just telling the person to go here or there.

The sixth fruit we find is goodness. Goodness is reaching out to do good to others even when they do not deserve it. This means that as an usher or greeter, you must have a forgiving spirit without having to receive an apology from some people. Goodness involves looking beyond the wrong that was done to you. Just as Christ took our sins upon himself, excelling ushers and greeters take the wrong of others upon themselves. Yes, they may not deserve what you're going to do for them, but go ahead and do it anyways because it is the right thing to do. Your goal is to always serve in a manner that is pleasing to Christ.

The seventh fruit we find is faithfulness. Your faithfulness is not just an act of service to the church; it is actually your service to God. Are you a dependable member of your team at your post at the times you are assigned? Remember, Jesus told you that if you are faithful in the little things, you will also be faithful in much. As an usher or greeter you want to make sure that you are trustworthy, reliable and dependable in your service.

The ninth fruit we find is gentleness. You are called to have a humble spirit that is in submission to God and to God's word at all times. In those moments when you feel anger is rising up within you, you are to allow the Holy Spirit to keep that anger in check. Recall, with all that Moses did in putting up with the children of Israel and all their complaints and rebellion, it was Moses' action of striking the rock in a moment of anger that kept him out of the Promised Land. There will be moments in which you are frustrated by people's blatant disregard for the rules of the church. But remember, the anger of people does not achieve the righteousness that God has for their lives. You have a higher calling on your life than to let anger control you in your position.

The tenth and final fruit we find is self-control. You will manifest this fruit best by subjecting yourself to prayer and the will of God, before you assume your post. Pray, "Lord, how do you want to use me today to help someone be drawn closer to You? Ushers and Greeters must understand that it is not all about them when they are at their post. The goal is to always help find a way to make it easier for someone to experience the love and grace of God while maintaining order in the worship service.

Let This Fruit Be Born In You!

- *Love*
- *Joy*

- *Peace*
- *Patience*
- *Kindness*
- *Goodness*
- *Faithfulness*
- *Gentleness*
- *Self-Control*

Tasks To Be Performed

1 Corinthians 12:4-6 (KJV) [4] Now there are diversities of gifts, but the same Spirit. [5] And there are differences of administrations, but the same Lord. [6] And there are diversities of operations, but it is the same God which worketh all in all.

Each church will have its own specific rules for ushers and greeters regarding which job duties will be assigned to the groups. Here are some tasks that are common to many ushers and greeters, even though the form they take will vary slightly from church to church. Ushers and greeters are at the forefront of a church's ability to do follow-up to all guests.

Most churches have some type of visitor or guest card that the church wants filled out in order to get information concerning the person's address, phone number and e-mail. These cards are of immense value in being able to contact people once they have left the service to thank them for coming. They can also be used to invite the person back for special events throughout the year. The cards are one of the pillars in helping your church to grow.

Ushers and greeters are in the most strategic place to personally ask guests to fill out a card. It is good to have pens or pencils on you, so that when you pass out a guest card, you may also give them the pen or pencil to complete the information. Be clear to the guest what they are to do with the card. Do they put it in the offering basket? Do they give it to an usher? Do they put it in a special box? Make it clear, and don't be afraid to ask a guest after service, "Did you have a chance to fill out a guest card." If your church has a guest welcome station in which they can pick up a gift, make sure you offer to take them to the welcome station after the service is over. Go looking for the guest in your church so as to help your church grow.

Many churches will have a sign in or attendance form for members and friends to check off so that the church can keep up with who has been missing. Ushers and greeters can be very helpful in making sure people check off their names if they have bypassed the sign in list. At our church, our ushers and greeters will offer to check off a person's name as the person passes by. Some people have a hard time seeing and greatly appreciate having the usher or greeter find and check off their names for them.

In addition to the attendance form, many churches request that their ushers and greeters count the number of people who are actually in worship for each Sunday. The number should include children and adults. The number may be broken down by the number of people in the sanctuary, the number of people in youth church, and the number of people in the nursery. However the count is done, it should be done consistently each week and the number should be recorded on a specific form that is set out in the same place each week.

Another important card for churches to have is a card that explains what the Nursery policy is and what youth or children's church is about. Parents need to know what time the nursery starts and end and what the age group is for kids in the nursery. They also need to know where the nursery is located. A picture of the nursery on the card will help the parents to decide whether or not to take their kids to the nursery.

In today's age of child abuse, some parents will be reluctant to leave their children in the nursery with total strangers. Our church has video cameras covering the nursery area so that parents can see the nursery, before being asked to take their children to the nursery. If the church has a policy of no babies or toddlers in the sanctuary, it should be stated on the card. The directions to the alternative space for parents who do not want to leave their kids in the nursery should also be on the card. This prevents people from thinking you have something just against them. Remember, guests want to make sure their children are going to be safe, so there should always be some adults supervising the nursery.

Many churches may have children's church or youth church. They differ on how it operates. In some churches, kids go straight to youth church, in other churches kids are dismissed after a certain event in the regular worship service. Passing out a card to guests with kids about youth church can be very helpful. The card should inform parents of the ages for youth worship, where classes are held, when it starts and when it will be over.

Most churches will distribute a bulletin or program which includes the order of service for the worship service and various announcements. Ushers and greeters should never hand these items out without making eye contact with the person receiving it along with giving them a smile and a friendly greeting. You want the person to be as prepared as possible for the worship service. If your program is not easily understandable, then let your guest know how to follow it along. As you are looking over the sanctuary during worship, keep your eyes open for people who may not have received a bulletin and take one to them.

Churches have various traditions concerning the use of candles in the service. Sometimes candles are lit throughout the service. In some situations, the ushers and greeters are expected to light the candles. Often times this will be done prior to the start of the service. You need to know who is responsible for lighting the candles and who is responsible for putting them out at the end of the service.

Ushers and greeters are also needed for homegoing services, funerals and memorial services held in churches. When you hear of a service being scheduled at your church, if possible, you should offer your services to help out.

Many of the tasks that you do on a Sunday morning will be required at a funeral service. You will have far more guests at your church who will need directions concerning going from place to place in your building. You will also have a larger percentage of unchurched people in the audience. Your acceptance of them may be a gateway opening to the Spirit speaking to their hearts during the service. People are going to judge your church by the way they are treated by the ushers and greeters.

Ushers and greeters function as a part of a team. You should have something on your clothing that helps others to identify you as an usher or greeter. It could be a button, a badge, a ribbon, or a smock. The identification will help your guests to feel more at ease as you approach them or as they approach you. If your ushers and greeters have special colors for certain Sundays, be a team player and make sure that you are appropriately dressed.

Seating And Latecomers

Acts 5:6-7 (KJV)[6] And the young men arose, wound him up, and carried him out, and buried him.[7] And it was about the space of three hours after, when his wife, not knowing what was done, came in.

Churches will have different policies on seating of people as they enter the sanctuary. Some churches allow people to sit wherever they would like to sit, while other churches have a firm policy of filling in each row and seat before allowing others to choose the next row. It is your job to know what your church's policy is so that you can be consistent in carrying out your duties.

If your church's policy allows people to sit where they like, you should ask guest, "How far down would you like to sit?" Regular members will often have a specific section they want to sit in, and they will remain consistent for the most part to that area. You should lead them down the aisle to their seats as well.

One of the things that ushers want to avoid is having new guests sit in areas of the church where they will be isolated from everyone else. If there is a section of the church that you know will be empty, but a guest has set in that area, be pro-active and let them know why you are suggesting they move to another section. If your church has a tradition of saving certain sections for the choir, the mothers, the deacons, or whatever, do not allow a guest to sit in those areas and then be embarrassed by others telling them to move. An excelling usher handles seating in the most kind and diplomatic of ways. Do not lead guests to seating where they are being asked to climb over people to get to a seat. If you must do it, then you should be the one to ask people already seated to either slide down, or to make way for the guests. Many people are just not smart enough to make the move to slide down on their own.

We have an increasing number of people who are entering our churches through wheelchairs, and that's good news. You should know the wheelchair accessible entrance into your sanctuary from your parking lot. We want to make everyone feel comfortable. There should be a section of your sanctuary in which a wheelchair will fit. There should be seats in the area for the people who are with the person may also sit. The area should be in the middle of your sanctuary if possible so that the person in the wheelchair will be surrounded by others. You do not want to make your very last row the only area available for wheelchairs if at all possible.

Be thoughtful of your guests. If you know there is a section of your church that is more disruptive because of people talking to each other, do not seat your guest in that area. Sometimes certain adults will talk to each other way too much during the service or sometimes teens will gather in a certain section and do the same thing. It is fine to ask both groups to please stop talking. I once had a couple visit our church who told me afterwards, they enjoyed the service, but they would not be back because of the group behind them that kept talking throughout the service. But be pro-active and seat your guests in a better area. You usually will only have this problem in an open seating church.

Keep in mind that if someone comes in with a baby or toddlers, you want to seat them in an area where they can be removed with the least amount of distraction if the child starts crying. Where you seat them is going to depend on the design of your church. If the exit or the space reserved for parents and infants is near the front of the sanctuary, then they should be seated near the front, but if the area is located near the rear of the sanctuary, then they should be seated near the rear.

Once the pastor has started preaching, do not lead a guest or anyone else to the front of the church to be seated. That is distracting for both the speaker and the audience. If the church does have an open seating policy, try to fill in the seats closest to the front first. It will make your church look and feel fuller and it will help the speaker psychologically.

If you know your church is going to be less than three quarters full, block off or rope off the last few rows of pews to keep anyone from sitting in them. Of course this will give you an opportunity to practice your gentleness because someone is going to move the rope just to sit in the back. Do not give up on roping off the back just because a few persons will not want to comply. Your long range goal is to help make your church as attractive to guests as you can possibly make it.

Churches will differ on their protocol of when people may enter the service once a service has begun. Remember, ushers want to maintain order in the service so that those in the service can have the most meaningful worship experience possible. This means not allowing the flow of the service to be interrupted by the distractions of others. In general, ushers should not allow seating to take place during times of prayer, during the Scripture reading, during solos, dances, or choir selections. Some churches forbid people to enter the sanctuary once the sermon has begun. Ushers should be on hand to direct people to the alternative spot in the building where people may then listen to the sermon.

People should be allowed to enter during congregational singing, announcements being made, and transitions between one part of the service to another. Churches are somewhat divided on whether or not to allow individuals to enter during the time the offering is being received. You need to learn the protocol of your particular congregation to know what other parts of your services you do not allow latecomers to enter the sanctuary.

Some people will be tempted to get up and walk out of the service during the very times people should not be walking. Do not confront the people as they are leaving the seat. You do not want to be a bigger disturbance to the worship service than was the person who got up to exit Let your gentleness come to the forefront and speak to the person after they have exited the sanctuary to let them know, what the rules of the church are. Sometimes the person will apologize and indicate they're sorry and were unaware of the rule. There will be times when the person will not appreciate the reminder. This again is why patience has to be one of the fruit in an excelling usher's or greeter's life.

Some people will have legitimate health reasons for why they will need to leave the service each week on a regular basis. It may be due to medicine or pain. Try to work out a seating arrangement in which their leaving will cause as little disruption as possible.

People should not be allowed to exit the building in a way that takes them across the front of a speaker or group singing. Ushers should never lead people across the front of a speaker unless that is the only possible way to leave the worship area. As doorkeepers in the house of the Lord, it is very important for those functioning as ushers to carry out their jobs faithfully.

The Pastors

2 Timothy 4:11 (KJV)[11] Only Luke is with me. Take Mark, and bring him with thee: for he is profitable to me for the ministry.

Ushers and greeters should realize that they are also called to be ministering servants to the pastors during the worship service. In many churches ushers and greeters are responsible for putting out water for the pastor and other speakers prior to the start of service. Ushers are the only ones who can simply get up and walk at any time during the service. This makes them a valuable asset to the pastors

There should be at least one usher who is always cognizant of the pastor. If the pastor needs to get a message across to someone, he or she is going to need to have the attention of an usher. A simple nod or finger action to come forward should deliver an usher to the pastor.

Ushers should be proactive with the pastor as well. If the pastor's voice is cracking, take some water up to him or her. If the pastor has a cold while speaking, be sensitive to see if the pastor may need some Kleenex tissues. If the pastor has some kind of sermon props for the message, be ready to bring items forward or assist with moving items. Your heart as a servant should kick in, and you should be ready to serve as needed.

The temperature in the sanctuary will greatly influence the ability of the congregation to hear the word of God. If a sanctuary gets too warm, and there is no circulation of air, people are going to start to fall asleep regardless of the sermon content. Ushers can help the pastors out in this situation. The pastors may need for the heating in the building to be turned down or up. The air conditioning may need to be turned on or off. The fans may need to be turned on or off. The ushers and greeters should know where the controls to each of these things are located so that they can carry out the desires of the pastors. Excelling ushers will anticipate some of these problems and begin to take action, even before the pastor requires their attention.

Disruptions In The Service

3 John 1:9-10 (KJV)[9] I wrote unto the church: but Diotrephes, who loveth to have the preeminence among them, receiveth us not. [10] Wherefore, if I come, I will remember his deeds which he doeth, prating against us with malicious words: and not content therewith, neither doth he himself receive the brethren, and forbiddeth them that would, and casteth them out of the church.

Part of the ushers and greeters job is to assist in making sure the service flows as smoothly as possible. This is not always going to be as easy as it looks, because at times it means dealing with situations the usher or greeter would rather not have to confront. You will have your share of uneasy moments in which others will be thinking, "Why doesn't the ushers do something?"

One of the most common disruptions is babies crying during the service and parents not removing them from the service. The church needs to have established a place in the building where parents can take their children who are crying. Just think, a pastor spends hours preparing a message or a choir spends hours rehearsing for a song. All that effort can go down the tubes with a screaming baby and a parent refusing to take the child out of the sanctuary. The work of the Holy Spirit in some people's heart comes to a grinding halt.

Each church should have a policy on parents who choose not to take their kids to the nursery, and the policy should be written on a card which encourages parents to utilize the nursery. If guests do enter the sanctuary with infants and toddlers, you should make sure they receive a card concerning the nursery. The card should have on it, that parents whose children begin to cry, must immediately take their children out of the sanctuary, and where it is they are to go. This will make the ushers' job much easier.

When the child begins to cry, the usher should go immediately to the parent, and tell them, "Please follow me to the parent-child area." Remember that if you do not act, some people will not know where to take their child, so they will simply stay in the sanctuary. Some parents will appreciate your presence to help provide them a way of escape. Some will not and try to insist the child is going to stop crying in a second. It is not fair to the congregation that has come seeking to hear from God, to have to listen to a crying baby or acting out toddler. You can help diffuse the situation by speaking in a loving and gentle voice when telling the parents to please follow you.

The other common disruption in the service will be adults talking to each other and teens or youth gathering in one area to talk with each other. Your job is to speak to the group and remind them that their behavior is keeping others from hearing from God. If you have spoken to the group on more than one occasion, you should let the pastor or the leadership know of the problem. In the case of the youth, you may have to request they sit with a parent, or have an elder or deacon sit among them. Remember to handle yourself with grace in the situations. It will help if you can speak to the person or youth by their name. Emphasize respecting the rights of those who are trying to draw closer to God.

You may have the situation arise in which someone needs medical help during the service. If possible, try to lead the person outside of the sanctuary and dial 911 for assistance. Ushers and greeters are to be looking over the congregation to be alert to any medical problems which may be taking place. You know that you have done your job well, when a medical emergency arises, but very few of the people in the service actually knew there was a problem.

You may have the intentional disruptive person who enters your service keeping a lot of noise. It is best if you have several men in your church that can surround the person and remove the person from the sanctuary as quickly as possible. Overcome the person with the number of people surrounding them. There may be times the men will have to forcibly remove the person, but it is always best to give the person space to walk out on their own.

You will sometimes encounter a situation in which you should prevent a person from entering the sanctuary because of the way they smell. Sometimes people will use their odor as a means to get money out of you for them to leave. If a person has a very strong odor, it will spread to those around them and they will be hindered in their ability to worship. Depending on the type of seating you have, the odor may persist in the seats long after the person is gone. It is better to minister to this person one on one.

Ushers and greeters will need to be honest with the person and let the person know, they will be allowed in the sanctuary if they want to return, but they cannot enter in smelling as they smell. No doubt some people will think this is an un-Christian position, but if the person came to learn about Christ, the person should be willing to listen to someone talk to them one on one about Christ. If the person indicates he came to give his life to God, he can give his life to God in a classroom as well as in a sanctuary.

We are living in age of increasing violence taking place in the church. Ushers and greeters have to be more diligent than ever detecting people acting suspiciously in church. Shootings and child abductions at churches are becoming more frequent. Ushers may want to have a church lockdown strategy in place should gunshots be heard in the church or on church property. Churches may need to consider the possibility of having some armed people at the church to stop violence that has started.

The Offering

2 Corinthians 9:6-7 (KJV)[6] But this I say, He which soweth sparingly shall reap also sparingly; and he which soweth bountifully shall reap also bountifully.
[7] Every man according as he purposeth in his heart, so let him give; not grudgingly, or of necessity: for God loveth a cheerful giver.

Taking up the offering is no longer as simple as it used to be. Today some people give their offering through online giving, text giving, bank mailed issued checks, as well as the traditional offering plate. It's hard to know who has given their offering before the service even started. So avoid making gossip type statements such as "Mr. Jones never puts anything in the offering plate."

Some churches have attempted to make the church seem less about money so they do not even take up an offering. Instead they leave offering boxes at the end of the last rows or at the doors for people to simply drop their offering in the box on their way out after service. There is no right or wrong way to receive the offering. Each church has to discover what it most effective for it.

Many churches use envelopes for people to give their offerings. This allows for them to keep a record of what people give, especially those who give cash. This also helps to remove the temptation some people have to take money out of the offering plate as it passes by. Not everyone sitting in church is honest, and there are those who do attempt to steal from the offering plate. Ushers should know where extra envelopes are kept in order to offer them to anyone who needs them.

Even though we have various electronic forms of giving available, most churches still rely on the offering plate for most of their collections. That means that ushers will continue to be needed to receive the offering. Churches have different protocols for ushers when it comes to taking up the offering. Some pray before the ushers receive the offering, and some pray after the offering is received. Some churches have the ushers start in the back and finish up front, and other churches do the exact opposite.

The goal should be to take up the offering as quickly and as efficiently as possible. The number of ushers needed will depend on the size and layout of the sanctuary as well as the number of people present in the service. Since ushers are to maintain decency and order in the service, the way in which they take up the offering should have some decency and uniformity about it.

If an offering plate is passed across a row, there should be an usher on each side of the row. One usher should send the offering container down the first row, while the other should send the offering container down the second row. The two ushers should remain even with each other as they continue the process of sending the containers down different rows at the same time.

What happens after all the ushers have received the offering is going to be determined by the protocol of the church.

Ushers must learn their church's protocol. There does need to be an understanding of who is to take the offering from the sanctuary, and where the offering is to go. There should be a minimum of two people taking the final offering to its destination. You want to be concerned with security and safety when it comes to transporting an offering. Minimize the risks in whatever way you deem necessary. Have some men along the route from the sanctuary to wherever the offering is taken. Although must offerings are in the form of checks, thieves are not always aware of it. Keep in mind that thieves rob banks and receive less in funds than is in many church offerings.

If an offering is collected outside the sanctuary, never send one person to receive that offering. For instance if an offering is taken in youth church or in an overflow room from them the main sanctuary, that is brought together with the offering in the sanctuary, send two people to get the other offerings. You do not want to put an usher in a position of being falsely accused concerning an offering. Nor do you want to put a needless temptation in front of anyone. Ushers should live beyond reproach when it comes to receiving the offering.

Where Are Those Things Located

Ephesians 6:10-12 (KJV) [10] *Finally, my brethren, be strong in the Lord, and in the power of his might.* [11] *Put on the whole armour of God, that ye may be able to stand against the wiles of the devil.* [12] *For we wrestle not against flesh and blood, but against principalities, against powers, against the rulers of the darkness of this world, against spiritual wickedness in high places.*

The more knowledgeable ushers and greeters are about their building and its contents, the more effective they will be as servants in their positions. The smaller a church is, the more knowledgeable ushers and greeters will have to be. Ushers and greeters should know where to locate the items that they will have to use in fulfilling their duties.

The bulletins or programs are a very important part of the ministry. Ushers and Greeters should take their posts no later than

15 to 20 minutes prior to the start of the service. Do you know where the programs are kept before the service? If they are locked up, is there at least one usher with a key to gain access to the programs.

The visitor or guest cards, the nursery cards, and youth church cards are all very important. Do you know where each set of these cards are actually stored in case you run out during the services? Do you know where the extra pens and pencils are kept in your church? Do you know where the attendance sheets are stored? Where is the attendance count sheet stored each week?

The offering cannot be taken up without the offering containers. Do you know where those containers are stored after worship? Do you know where the extra offering envelopes are located if you should run out. These are things that should be checked prior to the start of the service.

Having Kleenex tissues and hand fans can be a blessing to those in need. Do you know where to go to get extra tissues or who to talk to about them? Do you know where the hand fans are, and where they are stored after worship? Is it the ushers' and greeters' job to collect all the fans after worship and put them back in the proper place?

Do you know where the thermostat is to control the heating system? Do you know where the thermostat is to control the air conditioning? Who should you contact if you're at church early and the furnace or air conditioner is not working? Do you know where the fuse box is in case some of the outlets stop working during the service? Do you know where the switches are for the lighting in the building?

Being able to answer yes to all of these questions will make you a much more effective usher and greeter, while at the same time, making you much more valuable to the pastors. You can field answers to people's questions and request while allowing the pastors to continue on with other parts of the ministry during the worship service.

The Reason For It All

Colossians 3:15-17 (KJV) [15] *And let the peace of God rule in your hearts, to the which also ye are called in one body; and be ye thankful.* [16] *Let the word of Christ dwell in you richly in all wisdom; teaching and admonishing one another in psalms and hymns and spiritual songs, singing with grace in your hearts to the Lord.* [17] *And whatsoever ye do in word or deed, do all in the name of the Lord Jesus, giving thanks to God and the Father by him.*

Ushers and greeters serve in the life of the church because they want to make a difference in people's lives for the cause of Christ. You must see yourselves as a very important part of the body of Christ that is working together with the other parts of the body to lead people closer to God. A warm greeting upon arrival at the church can do as much to lift a person's spirit as a great solo that was sung by someone in the choir. The helpful deed done by an usher can cause someone to feel the presence of God just as much as the outstanding sermon preached from the pulpit.

Ushers and greeters must see yourselves as very important in the body of Christ. Someone has said, "It takes teamwork to make the dream work." Ushers and greeters should be eager to cover for each other when a helping hand is needed. God is calling you to excel in your ministry. As members of the same time, you must be supportive of each other. You must be dependable and reliable. Never simply abandon your post. If you cannot be present on your scheduled Sunday, do all that you can to find a replacement to stand in for you. If someone needs you to stand in for them, consider it an honor and privilege to do so and say yes when possible.

Always be on the lookout for others that you can recruit into this ministry. A church can never have enough excelling ushers and greeters. Remember that your outer ministry will only be effective as long as you are nourishing your own inner soul. Being an excellent usher and greeter requires that you miss being able to fully engage God in worship. So either attend another service at your church just for your own personal feeding, or watch a copy of the service on DVD or on your website.

God has called you to excel in going forward and to make a difference. It is a privilege to be a doorkeeper in the house of the Lord. Go ahead and lift the spirits of many people through your service. Now that you know what you are to do, go ahead and do it with all your might. The rest of the body of Christ is depending on you.

- Serve The Lord With Gladness
- Serve The Lord With Joy
- Serve The Lord With Faithfulness
- Serve The Lord With Praise
- Serve The Lord With Endurance
- Serve The Lord With Purpose
- Serve The Lord With Your Whole Being

Acknowledgment By The Author

Thank you for taking the time to purchase this book. The goal of this book is to produce excellence in your usher and greeter ministry. If you are just starting as a church, this book provides teaching and instruction for ushers and greeters, as well as providing insight and solutions to problems that are going to arise in the life of the church. It provides examples of how different churches handle different situations so that you can choose the method which will be most effective for you. This book is helpful for any usher and greeter to read so as to become more effective in the ministry God has for them. Ushers and greeters are very important in the life of the church. I pray that this book will be a blessing to you and your church.

Sincerely

Rick Gillespie-Mobley

rickntoby@yahoo.com

newlifeatcalvary.org

attorneyrgm@gnlcc.com

Other Books By The Author

The Screwtape Orders

Is God In The Crisis

20 Small Group Bible Studies

Growing In Christ Through The Book Of James: 12 Bible Studies

Eulogy How To Write Great Eulogies

Black History Sermons

Easter Holy Week Sermons

Father's Day Or Men's Day Sermons

Mother Day Sermons

36527915R00053

Printed in Great Britain
by Amazon